John Blakemore
British Image 3
Editor: Barry Lane, Photography Officer
Editorial Committee: Bill Gaskins, Victor Burgin, David Hurn,
Ron McCormick, Aaron Scharf, Peter Turner and Marina Vaizey
Editorial Assistant: Paul Blatchford
Design: Emanuel Sandreuter
This book was printed in Stonetone by Rapoport Printing Corp., New York.
Distributed by Gordon Fraser, Fitzroy Road, London NW1 8TP
© 1977 Arts Council of Great Britain
Introduction © Gerry Badger

ISBN 0 7287 0107 3

British Image is published regularly by the Arts Council of Great Britain.
Individual copies or regular orders may be obtained from the Publications
Office. A list of Arts Council publications, including all exhibition
catalogues in print, can also be obtained from the Publications Office,
Arts Council of Great Britain, 105 Piccadilly, London W1V 0AU.

BRITISH IMAGE 3

John Blakemore

Introduction by Gerry Badger

Arts Council of Great Britain 1977

For Penelope

Introduction by Gerry Badger

An intrinsic love for the land and an inherent respect for nature are generally regarded as a fundamental part of our national consciousness. Indeed, the landscape has been the primary subject of our greatest painters; it has inspired many of the most memorable flights of fancy of our greatest poets; and it has been a major preoccupation of our leading artistic and moral philosophers. But for all the persuasiveness of this great national myth – and whether a general truism or not it has effectively assumed the attributes of myth – the landscape has not, with a very few and singularly obvious exceptions, been an especially fruitful or notable field for British photographers.

Recently, however, photographers in this country have begun to approach the natural environment with renewed awareness. It is an awareness which stems both from a fairly widely felt need for man to establish a more intimate relationship with the land – the growing issue of ecology has imparted an even greater credence to the notion of nature as the residual font of pure, untainted spiritual values – and also from an expanded understanding of the medium: a realisation and utilisation of the photograph's propensity for signifying the 'felt' and the unseen as well as the seen.

John Blakemore's vision is a fusion of several distinct lines of thought, representing different facets of his own relationship with nature and his understanding of the potentialities of the still photograph. His pictures are at the same time an attempt to define and to quantify a personal contact with the fabric of nature, and to explore natural processes as manifest in the cycles of growth, decay, death, regeneration and the physical forces which shape the landscape – wind, water, sun and frost. His iconography is a reflection of himself in nature, a reflection of his own spiritual need to determine a deeper and more lasting reconciliation with existence than that provided by the fragile, everyday realities of urban living and the rigours of establishing often all too transient human relationships. In a wider sense he is reaffirming not only his own but man's place in the natural order – an affirmation of the essential continuity of man and nature and a timely reminder of the interrelatedness of all things, ignored by profligate modern man at his peril.

His personal affirmation is deceptively simple, but fundamental. 'The basic reason that I make landscape photographs is that I love the landscape.' This love of the landscape is a deeply rooted instinct in John Blakemore, although it was only around 1968 that it surfaced in his photography, when he became aware of it as a powerful force in his psyche and glimpsed in it the potential direction of his future creative work. At that time he had been working as a commercial photographer, but had temporarily given up work to go to Wales for the winter. It was the kind of sabbatical period that we all need from time to time. His life was at a low ebb for he was experiencing the traumas of the break-up of his first marriage, but he found a profound consolation in the emptiness and solitude of the Welsh landscape, and the whole experience became a spiritual rebirth. He did not actually photograph then – the experience seemed too vast, too important to put down on a sheet of photographic paper – but he wrote about the landscape, he walked into the landscape, and he became very close to the landscape. 'I walked up into the mountains sat on the rocks and just listened to the wind.'

This intimacy with nature and with the landscape has become the primary force behind his photography although in effect it is a very personal, totally private impulse, a physical, almost sensual emotion, and as such is not readily translatable into photographic images. Indeed, it took him some two years after the Welsh sojourn to make pictures stemming from the insights of that trip, and there are times still now when the physical experience overwhelms – like the ten days spent camping alone on Cape Wrath which yielded only one, though memorable, image. Yet he seeks to quantify and to communicate that experience through the medium of the photograph and in this, of course, John Blakemore has all the natural urge of the image-maker. But to him the medium is more valuable; for the camera serves him not only in the role of a mnemonic or a surrogate for a perceived experience – the camera image opens up new directions, new areas of experience. It is a self-feeding, two-way process.

So, the act itself of making the photograph must be an integral part of, and not an intrusion into, his wider experience of the land. The moment of taking must flow out of a moment of oneness with nature; the creation of the image must become a perfect product of and expression of the photographer's harmony with the natural fabric. John Blakemore's images are not won lightly, they are the result of a long process of coming to terms with himself and the places he chooses to photograph, of watching, waiting and listening, of tuning his mind to that special state of blank awareness which Minor White has defined. Blakemore himself describes the development of this inner state:

'I began to have the kind of experience which became very important in my later work, a sort of total loss of myself in *my* work. It became very much a process of contemplation where I would lose myself in the photography for a long period and this experience of oneness with nature became very important to me. The most fruitful periods of work now are when this happens, so I try to find ways of making it happen more frequently.'

'When I begin to photograph now, I begin with a period of – not quite meditation – but almost. I sit in silence with my eyes closed and I listen to the sound of the place and try to become as much as I can part of the place that I'm in.'

Thus place becomes fundamentally important to John Blakemore, for again his interaction with nature is a two-way process and it is only in certain places that he feels the spiritual mutuality necessary for the making of his images. He is not interested in place in a topographical sense, but certain areas exert a powerful fascination upon him, and he will return to work in these locations again and again. There is, for example, a small stream in Derbyshire. It *is* a small stream, merely a yard or two wide, yet it forms the subject of two major sequences in this volume. He has photographed it assiduously for a number of years yet still has not reached its source. He knows the sections he has photographed so well that each time he returns he knows if a rock has been displaced during the intervening passage of time.

Such is the degree of intimacy that he cultivates with the special places which move him to photograph. But what are the particular qualities which hold him, and draw him again and again? Many artists and photographers have felt affinities with special places, places where they may 'see' – in the widest sense of the word – rather than just 'look'. The painter Paul Nash described the emotions evoked by such a place as 'this "unreality", or rather this reality of another aspect of the accepted world, this mystery of clarity that is at once so elusive

and so positive'. These are, of course, highly intuitive, deeply psychological urgings – in most cases centred largely around the divination of a mythological 'spirit of place'. In John Blakemore's case, the mythology is quite specific; the essence of his searching is for the places where he may feel the energy-flow of the landscape. This is the specific root of his involvement with the land, and therefore of his photographic imagery.

John Blakemore then, uses the camera to record the natural objects he observes, not merely as objects but as processes. He is concerned with signifying, through the agency of an intense, sensitive scrutiny of the actual fabric of nature, the order of existence – the fecundity and tenacity of life, the intense struggle to grow and survive. Thus the contortions of rock and tree forms moulded by time and the elemental forces, or the molten flow of a stream delicately traced in time by a long time-exposure, symbolise the rhythms and quantify the forces of the natural cycle, and echo the ravages wrought by existence upon nature and upon man. Thus his mode of expression is not only literal but metaphorical, and the primary philosophical tenet in his work is the credo propounded by Alfred Stieglitz, developed and propagated by Minor White, and termed 'Equivalence'.

Equivalence is a specific exploration of the metaphorical potentiality of the still photograph, and represents not so much a methodology, but rather an increased appreciation of the symbolic potency of that which the camera may reveal. So, for John Blakemore, the concept of equivalence operates at several levels. Firstly, the factual – the straightforward though extremely intense transcription of the thing itself. Secondly, the formal metaphor – the poetic signification of formal and spatial elements. Thirdly – and this is perhaps the most difficult level, certainly the most personal – the emotional/spiritual experience, evoked by the image in both photographer and viewer, where the process not only of taking but of viewing becomes a new and wholly creative event.

These equivalent meanings may not, of course, be completely present at all levels in each individual image. The photographer builds up the layers of meaning in sequential groups of prints; each image then interacts with the others in the sequence, creating further layers of meaning – rather in the manner of a visual poem. Each sequence itself may concentrate upon just one or two aspects of layered meaning: it may be constructed in a static or a dynamic way, or employ a counterpoint of interacting and contrasting meanings. In short, the sequence gives the photographer command of an expanded language, a complex, coherent and refined language which affords a high degree of communication with the attuned viewer.

The first and most immediate level at which one may approach John Blakemore's vision has a factual, physical basis. As I have stressed, the root of his involvement with the landscape lies in the strength of his awareness of the natural forces manifest in a specific location – a particular rushing, tumbling, foaming stream, a singular still, silent, ancient glade, a distinctive bleak, snowbound, windswept gulley. So, the primary characteristic of most of his images is their intense, close physical contact with the actual fabric of nature. The overwhelming sensation is tactile. The sense of being able almost to feel the roughness of bark, the velveteen of moss, the veining of a leaf, the wet, cold smoothness of rock, the pull of surging water: such qualities are felt more keenly in Blakemore than in perhaps any other landscape photographer. They are a direct transcription of the kind of experiences that he has felt. Thus the texture of natural objects, delineated so precisely by the resolving capacities of the large format camera, signify quite literally the intimacy of his relationship with nature; but they also point to other levels of meaning, for they are the external, perceptible signs of the invisible forces which mould and shape the land.

It is the unseen, yet felt power of nature which we may perceive when we read John Blakemore's imagery at the second level of equivalence. Here, he is concerned primarily with two interrelated yet distinct strands of expression: firstly, with symbolising natural forces in an almost dimensional sense – exploring the energy-rhythms and temporal processes inherent in the continual flux of nature; and secondly, affirming the essential unity of nature, the mutual interaction of all living things.

These ideas are communicated by his intuitive, yet deliberate exploitation of the camera's intrinsic power to transcribe yet transfigure concrete actuality. He employs the subtle, shifting, sometimes accidental forms which only the camera may reveal to imply the constant metamorphosis effected by natural forces and by the life cycle. Nothing is what it seems. The natural object is not a static, finite entity, but merely a state: an expression of a tiny part of a larger event, and charged with a precognition of the states which both precede and follow it. The forces of nature fuse and mould all natural things. In recognition of this John Blakemore uses the implied existence of an opposing state or quality to heighten our experience of immediate reality. By signifying life he implies and thus signifies death, and so on, with growth and decay, destruction and regeneration, tranquility and struggle.

In the fluid, textural patterns of a rushing stream, traced by a long time-exposure, we may feel the surging rhythms of one of nature's most powerful forces. The fragile, delicate traceries created by melting ice are a reminder of the slow, but inexorable forces of erosion and disintegration. The simple play of light on a rock, caught by the camera, serves to melt the stone: it shimmers and glows and becomes translucent, almost vitrified – we glimpse the subterranean, heaving core of the earth itself. Within certain images, we may perceive anthropomorphic forms, the features of strange, shadowy, half-revealed animals which may suggest an actual physical manifestation of a 'spirit of place'. The natural world of John Blakemore is a paean of metamorphosis – solid becomes void and void becomes solid; viscous becomes fluid and fluid becomes viscous; inanimate becomes animate and animate becomes inanimate. In all, the photographer has woven a web of suggested states of formal and psychological change, sufficient to permit an imaginative wandering through his imagery. Thus precise, programmatic interpretations are not a necessity – indeed are not even desirable. For, although he has transcribed a physical actuality, John Blakemore has, more importantly, distilled the kind of imaginative experience that one may have when contemplating the infinitely variable forms of clouds or the flickering flames of a fire.

The visionary processes created in the viewer's mind by the gradual building up of formal metaphors are stimulated to an even greater degree at the third level of equivalence. Here, the metaphor becomes more abstruse: less directly related to subject matter on a literal, consciously public level; and much more meaningful at a private, unconscious level. The photograph reflects the photographer's total emotional experience at the time of taking, becoming the starting point for much deeper and broader flights of imagination. It is an object for meditation and a creative experience in itself.

This spirituality is present to one degree or another in all John Blakemore's work, but is most evident in *Premonitions*, the last – and the most personal and intimate – sequence in this volume. In this sequence we can trace many of the notational elements which occur elsewhere, but here a more intense poetry provides an overlay which we may only describe as mood. This poetry resonates with the deeply felt emotions of the photographer – his joys, desires, fears and hopes. Each sequence has its predominant and characteristic mood: *All Flows*, for example, is restless and energetic, while *Emergence* is peaceful, hopeful; yet in *Premonitions* the mood is perhaps deeper, pervading the image in a much more fundamental way, and therefore exemplifying more clearly this level of expression. It is a mood of foreboding, a darker mood which, although sometimes hinted at, generally was not expressed in the previous sequences. They epitomised the strength, the forcefulness and the very real power of nature, as does *Premonitions*, but their whole thrust was one of vigour, of hope, of those energies which, however robust and awesome, build and generate life. In *Premonitions* the mood has changed: the thrust is down. The viewer feels not the upward thrust of growth towards light and energy, but the suffocating, debilitating pull of the earth. He feels it in the claustrophobic atmosphere of dark, cold, windswept gullies; in the weight of the rock which holds down the single, forlorn tree struggling to escape and in the grip of the parasitic vine which slowly strangles the life from another. The emphasis is always upon the destructive forces of the life-cycle – death and decay. *Premonitions* reflects the melancholy side of John Blakemore, his guarded respect, his awe and sometimes his fear of nature, and also his view of the human predicament.

For the first time, also, a sign of man's pernicious hand intrudes directly into the natural scene. The sawn tree trunk is an obviously blunt reminder of man the destroyer. And so the oppressiveness of this sequence signifies quite clearly the oppressiveness of man himself – upon nature and upon his fellows. The mood therefore is elegiac, epitomised in the superb, contorted tree trunk, that incorporeal animal spirit which gazes wonderingly like a great, sad bull. The final image at last answers the question, and confirms the premonition which is always at the back of the viewer's mind and at the root of the sequence. A flat, grave-like rock is a reminder of that final pull of the earth, but as always in John Blakemore there is an inevitable, hopeful corollary: the tiny flowers pushing up through the rock affirm once more that death is only a state; it is not an end but a beginning.

Metamorphoses

Primal Surge

24

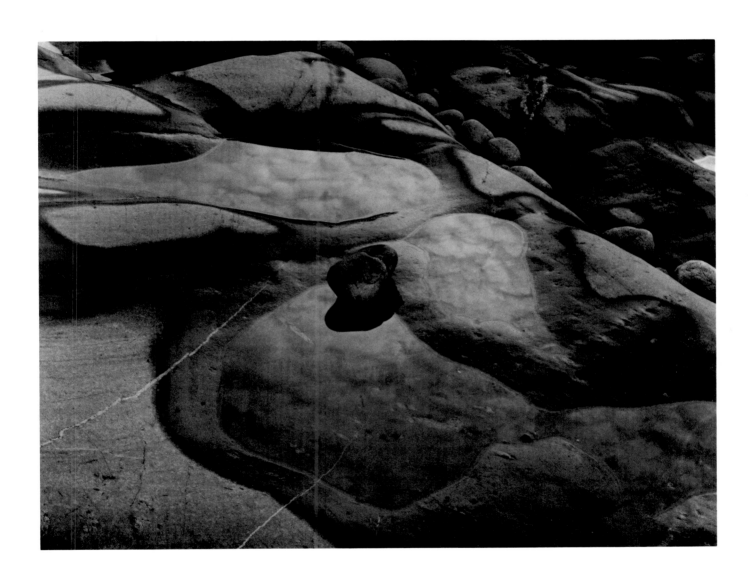

28

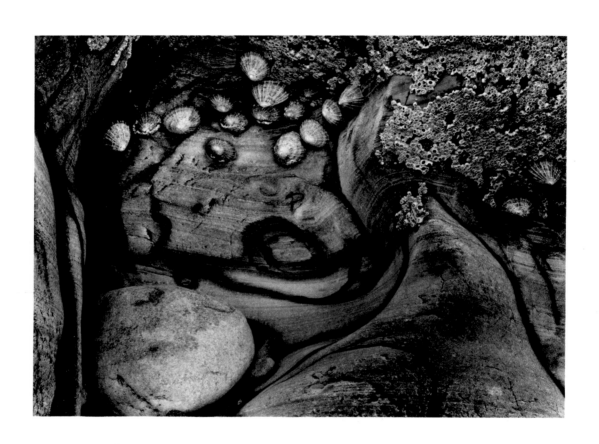

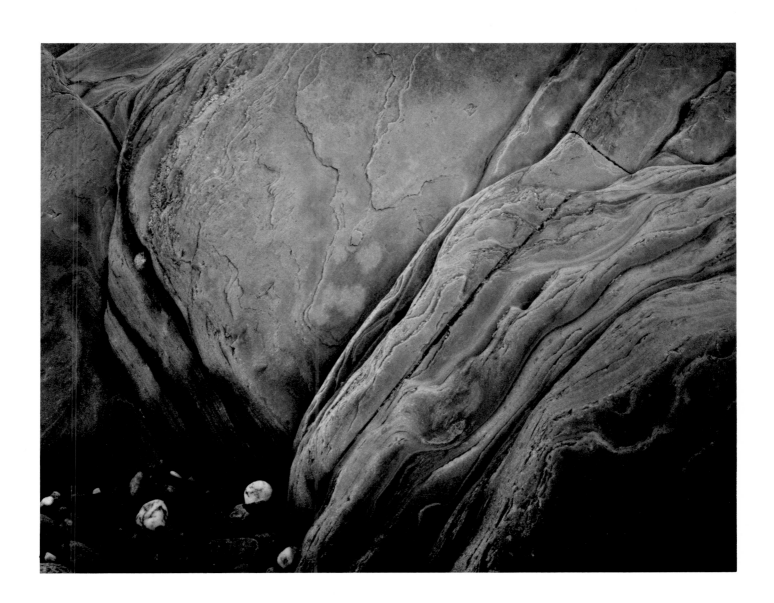

Emergence

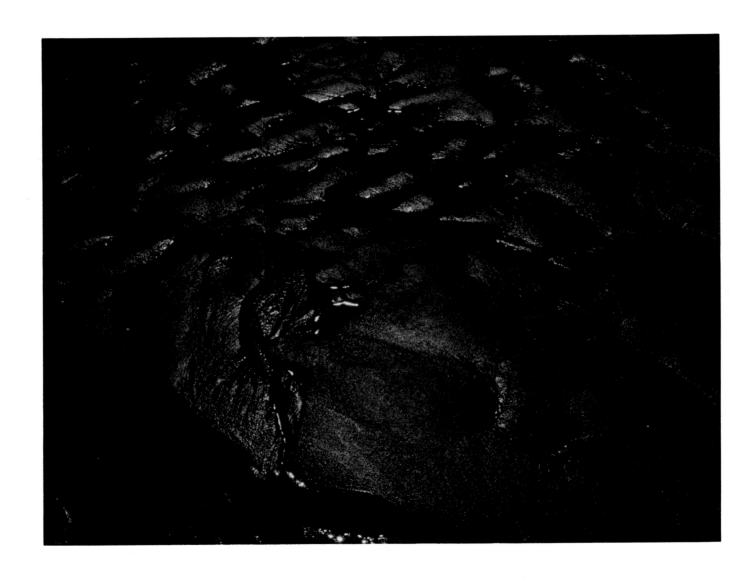

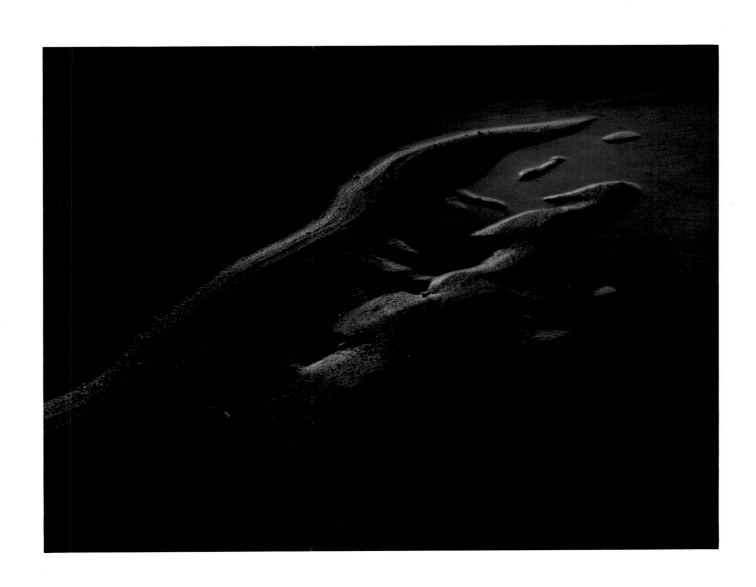

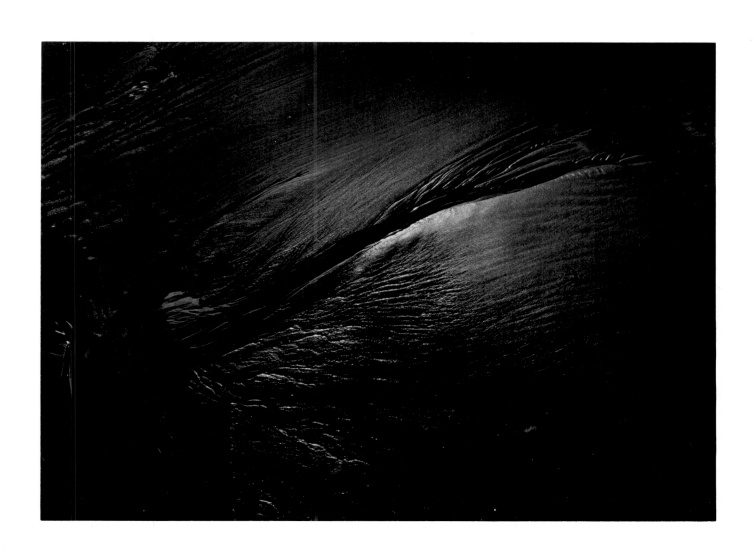

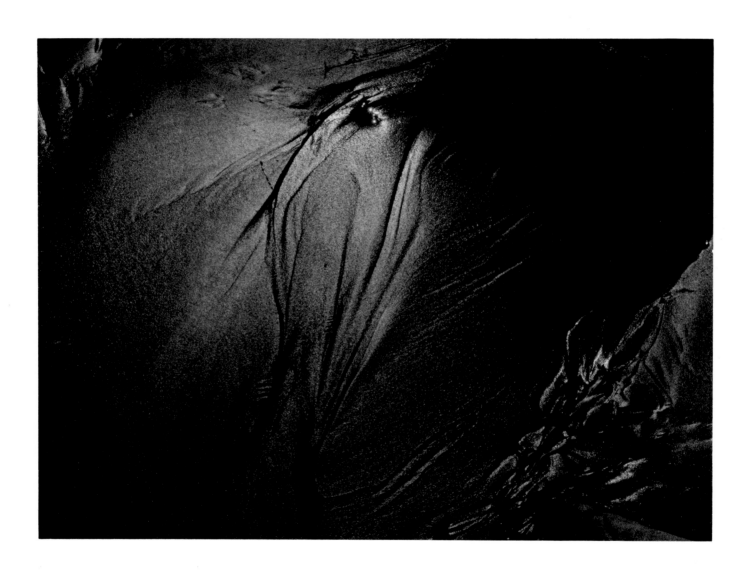

40

All flows

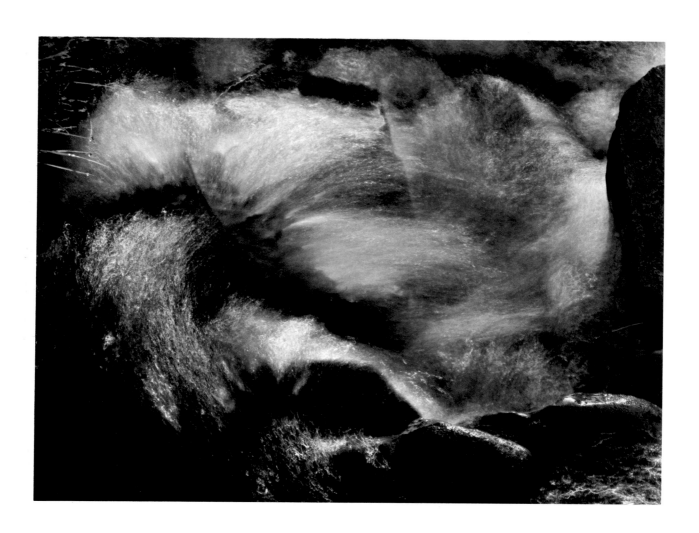

48

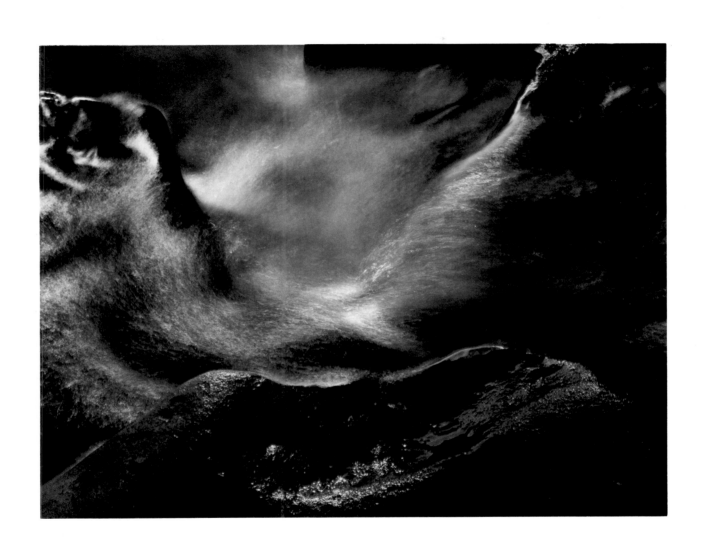

PREMONITIONS

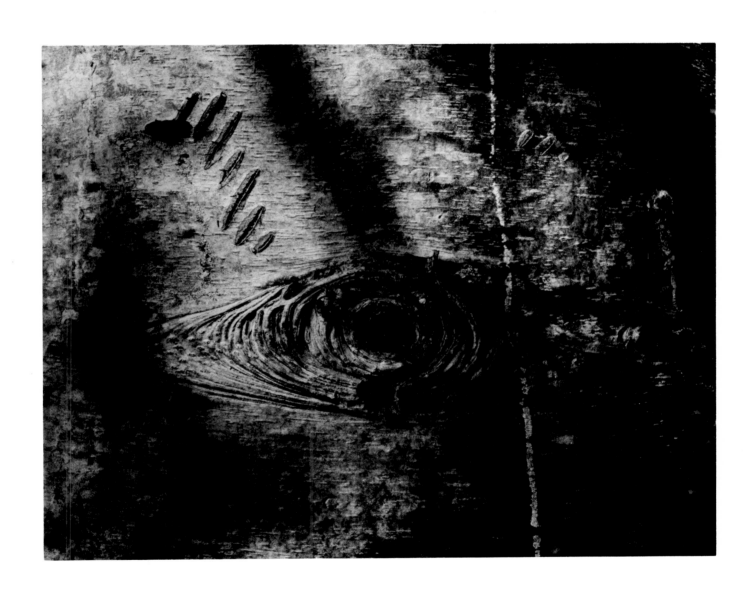